HARD LYING

By

GERALD URWIN

ACKNOWLEDGEMENTS.

Although the text is based primarily on Harold O'Neil's memory of what happened throughout his life, the background to events during the Second World War is provided by reference to the following :

1-The Second World War- Winston Churchill- Book Four – "The Hinge of Fate." Published by the Folio Society.

2- "Arctic Convoys 1941-1945"-Richard Woodman- Published by Pen & Sword.

3- "The Battle of the Atlantic"- Jonathan Dimbleby – publ. Viking.

4-" The Royal Naval Patrol Service" —- F.L.Fetherbe – publ. N.Kent Books.

5 –"Voices from the Arctic Convoys" Peter.C.Brown – publ. Stroud.

I would also like to thank Marie MacPherson for translating Russian texts, and Bill Rarity who provided great assistance with the pictures and presentation.

CONTENTS.

CHAPTER ONE.

EARLY DAYS.

The O'Neills have long been famous in Ireland folklore. Going all the way back to Brian O'Neill in the 13th century, Con O'Neill, clan leader in the 16th century, Owen Roe O'Neill, 1590 – 1649, a famous soldier, Hugh O'Neill, Earl of Tyrone, probably the most famous of them all, all the way up to modern times when we find Terence O'Neill, 1914-90, Prime Minister of Northern Ireland, the family has always been known for political and military skills, as leaders of men, and for showing a dash and verve sufficient to set them above their fellows.

Several of them, as was the case for many other Irish families, made a new start on the mainland, settling, for the most part, in Galloway in Scotland, and in the north east of England. It was there, at Annfield Plain in County Durham, on February 13th, 1922, that Harold O'Neill was born. Harold had an elder sister, Gladys, and, later, a younger brother, George. Dad was a butcher to trade, but switched to the more lucrative job of miner at the local "Busty" pit. There were also aunts, uncles, cousins in abundance, all living locally. Harold grew up as a well set-up lad, going to schools in Greencroft, Catchgate and Stanley, where his schoolmates , at school leaving age, were, for the most part, destined for a job underground, working in the huge Durham coalfield.

In the early years of his life, Harold was a happy youngster. With so many relatives there was always fun at hand, birthday parties to go to, adventure trips to join, grandparents, aunts and uncles to smile at him – he felt that he belonged to a group of loving people who would always care. His world crashed around him when, in 1929, grandparents, aunts, uncles and cousins emigrated en masse to Canada. Harold felt totally betrayed, especially when home life offered no replacement for his loss. Father was rarely to be seen, working long hours down the pit and only coming home in time to go to bed. His mother, who came from a disturbed family background, showed little affection for her children. There were no hugs, cuddles or kisses for them. Deprived of love, Harold became a changed character. The world had turned against him, so he would retaliate. He became aggressive. The school bully had a surprise when Harold, a much smaller lad, fought back fiercely. Harold had another scrap and , having floored his opponent, began to bang his head on the concrete playground. No one else took him on, recognising Harold's almost ungovernable bad temper.

Not for the last time, Harold chose an independent route. He was diagnosed as suffering from anhidrosis, the inability to perspire correctly. The treatment here offered did not always go according to plan. On one occasion, Harold mistakenly took a swig of a prepared solution which turned out to be dilute nitric acid. Fortunately he was caught in time , given the correct remedy, and recovered.

Treatment meant time lost at school, and spoiled Harold's chance of profiting from his formal education. He left school at 15 without any qualifications.

Harold favoured an open air life and occupation. After school, he took a job at the greyhound racing stadium at Stanley, Co. Durham. He looked after 20 dogs, before, during and following races. Greyhound racing attracted a huge audience as a welcome antidote to a life below ground for hard, grafting miners. Harold also took up hare coursing, but an inborn sense of adventure saw him set off for pastures new at the age of 16.

Mr Robinson, a neighbour worked in the engine house which operated the cage that took miners down and brought them back up at the Louisa pit in Stanley. His two sons looked after a retail business in Newcastle. They sold up and moved to London. Harold was offered the chance to work there. No doubt, Harold's heart skipped a beat. London! Sin City itself! What young man could resist the chance to see for himself if there was any truth in all of the stories of lurid goings-on in the capital city? Excited at the chance for a new start in life, Harold made his way to Marlborough Bus Station, in Newcastle and boarded the bus to London for the princely sum of £1. The journey took twelve hours.

Finding the place where he was hoping to work proved difficult. Harold did not know the geography of London at all. The size of the place was overwhelming. His knowledge of small Durham towns did not help in the slightest. He eventually sought help at Harrow on the Hill police station and was given directions to his destination, Kingsbury. Harold worked for the Jewish owner, Mr Tobias and then as a grocer in Mollison Way. He turned his hand to all jobs, nothing being too difficult for him, and proved a willing worker. He moved on to another grocery shop after a year, and became a canvasser for trade, encouraging housewives to use their ration books at his new employer's shop.

Harold wasted no time in discovering excitement and entertainment. He became a devoted fan of the theatre, especially the Palladium, where, for 14 shillings for a stall seat, he could laugh at the antics of The Crazy Gang (Nervo and Knox, Flanagan and Allen), the distinctive voices of Ivor Novello and Jack Buchanan, the harmony of Layton and Johnson, and many others. It was probably while admiring Jack Buchanan that Harold decided to copy his style of snappy dressing, a habit which has stayed with him throughout his life. So it was out with the "pullover" type of shirt and on with the new style American with buttons down the front. Of course, there was also the highly rated "Trilby" hat, although Harold later changed to a Homburg.

His progress in his new career was interrupted by a letter from his sister, Gladys, informing him of her forthcoming wedding. Harold left his job and returned north for the festivities, acting as his sister's Best Man.

His next journey took him southwards again, but, this time, only as far as York where he joined Rowntrees the famous chocolate and sweet manufacturer. The Rowntree family, Quakers and social reformers, were active pioneers in promoting labour welfare and education. Harold was soon employed in making wine gums. In his leisure time, he joined a harmonica band, most of whose members were employed by Rowntrees and usd their social club to practice, which was the start of a new career in entertainment.

From playing with the harmonica band Harold turned to singing in local pubs in the York area and developed a strong voice which later proved to be very useful in unexpected situations. Like all young men in England at the time, Harold considered serving in His Majesty's armed services. But which one? Unlikely though it may seem it was reading which confirmed his choice. Harold had taken out a book from the Catchgate library back home which was entitled "Under the White Ensign" by Percy F Westerman. From then on there could be only one choice for Harold. It was the Royal Navy for him. In 1940 he duly enlisted and waited, somewhat impatiently, to be called up for active service.

In the meantime he had a variety of jobs. He helped to open an army canteen, run by the NAAFI, in the Sheffield district. After the canteen was up and running satisfactorily a permanent staff took over while Harold and his workmates returned to York, working at the Railway Hotel. Then it was on to Lincoln where he found digs at Metheringham for the princely sum of three shillings a night, bed and breakfast. Another short stay, then back to York and work at Clifton airport where his manager was a former tea planter from India. Moving on to Harrogate, he found work at the Green Park Hotel in the kitchen before graduating to the splendid position of Hall Porter. A restless spirit caused him to leave for Tewkesbury and the job of wine waiter. There he nearly came a cropper when a dispute with the hotel manager resulted in a scuffle and the arrival of the police. After a dressing down and a cooling off period, the police let him go. Then on to Cheltenham and, finally, Leamington Spa where his newly married sister had set up home. Harold became a bus conductor on routes to Coventry, and from Warwick to Stratford on Avon.

By the time he had reached the age of 18, Harold was a tall 5feet nine and half inches with brown curly hair and a fresh complexion. He had rarely bothered to meet girls, either in London or elsewhere in the UK, but he was restless and uncertain of his future. Back home, in the summer of 1940, life changed for him completely. At a loose end, he had wandered over to Beamish Street, Stanley where an annual fairground was open for business. By chance a young girl was standing nearby watching a carousel as it whirled around with its complement of happy, screeching passengers. She was about five feet tall, a brunette and was smiling. Something sparked in Harold, and, totally out of character, he asked her if she would like to ride on the carousel. She agreed and the two of them took their places with the others. Afterwards Harold walked her home.

After saying goodnight Harold walked to the end
of the street where the girl lived, stopped, turned
round and made a silent promise to himself. "I
am going to marry that girl." That girl was
Beatrice Coxon and she became Harold's wife in
1944. The marriage was to last for sixty years.

Beatrice worked on the Team Valley estate, in
Gateshead, at a factory making shatter-proof
glass for use in military goggles as required by
the RAF and army drivers etc... Later in the war
years she was transferred to Coventry where she
was employed in stripping down the engines of
crashed aircraft for re-use in British aircraft.
Then began a long period of being apart, each
contributing in a small way to the war effort,
while waiting desperately for a letter containing
the latest news of their sweetheart. For Beatrice
the wait was probably more agonising,
especially when Harold was at sea. Shore leave
could bring respite but it was all over far too
quickly for each of them.

Harold was called up for service in the Royal
Navy in August 1941 and sent to Devonport for

training at HMS Raleigh. Ratings were assigned to firewatching duties in the naval warehouses for which they were supplied with a stirrup pump. A friend he met there told him about a new arm of the navy service which paid better. Accordingly Harold volunteered for the Royal Naval Patrol Service (R.N.P.S.) employing Skippers, mates and men of the Royal Naval Reserve. At the outset of war it listed six thousand men and six hundred vessels. Its range of duties was unspecified and, during the course of 1939-45, it fought in every theatre of war. Ships used were an assorted collection of trawlers and paddle steamers armed with WW1 guns and whatever weaponry could be commandeered. Fishermen formed the bulk of the crews but people, from all walks of life, including Harold, joined in the fun. Harold served in the RNPS from December 1940 until May 1946.

The Headquarters was a former municipal pleasure ground at Lowestoft which was duly called the "Sparrow's Nest." The camp adjoining consisted of twenty wooden huts in which the men were given lectures on seamanship, signalling, gunnery, boating as well as taking part in physical training. Wages were ten shillings a week. No leave was given. Harold was issued with a rifle and 40 rounds of ammunition and told to mount guard over the fish boxes ! He slept in the former concert hall. Harold was in the guard when he was told to report to the stores where he was given a supply of white uniforms. The implications were enormous. He went to see the Commander and told him it was no use sending him anywhere where it was likely to be hot. The Commander at first, told Harold he must obey orders but Harold replied that he was a Volunteer then detailed his inability to perspire problem, which is called anhidrosis. The Commander said "Will you go to Russia, and when Harold replied "Yes" issued him a chit with which he was to select his kit ready for a voyage to the Arctic. Then Harold was sent to Barry in South Wales, to await further orders.

CHAPTER TWO.

THE REASON WHY.

By September 1941 the war was going badly for Russia. Most of the Ukraine had fallen to the Nazi invader, Moscow was under siege, there were panzers at the gates of Leningrad. In Stalin's (President of the USSR) words, Russia was faced by "a mortal menace." He complained bitterly that the German army could concentrate on the Eastern Front because the Western allies had not opened a second front, nor shown the slightest intention of doing so. Russia was left to face Nazi Germany "virtually alone" – again his words. Tanks, planes, guns and ammunition were needed desperately.

Although Churchill, UK Prime Minister, was reluctant to cede to Stalin's bluster, he was nevertheless worried that Russia might be on the point of seeking terms of surrender which would leave Germany able to turn its full force on the UK. A Japanese invasion in the Far East threatened British possessions and there was a desperate shortage of planes, tanks and other armaments with which to mount a realistic defence. He was also aware that the USA did not care about British colonies but wanted Germany kept at bay and fully occupied by the Russian army. America as yet had not entered the war as a combatant but Churchill was keen to see that they did so, as quickly as possible. At a Moscow Conference on the 29th September attended by senior representatives of Russia, United States and the United Kingdom, a package was thrashed out which would see Russian demands met, to the tune of military armaments worth £1 billion.

A supply route was discussed and finally decided upon. Convoys would sail around the North Cape and thence through the Arctic Ocean to Murmansk and later Archangel. All three nations would be represented in each convoy. It was agreed that winter was the best season to sail. Convoys were given a number preceded by PQ, the initials of Philip Quellyn Roberts, an Admiralty Planning Officer. Arctic clothing was supplied to each RN crew member consisting of fur lined duffel coats, two pairs of woollen long johns, a white polo necked jersey, thick mittens and sea boot socks.

For the first four to five months, starting in October 1941, all went well. Only one ship was lost. By March 1942, with convoys having to sail further and further south to avoid ice floes, they were within range of the German air force, stationed in Northern Norway. Thereafter it was a different story. Hitler had sent several of his largest battleships to Norwegian waters, both to offset any British invasion and to intercept convoys ferrying supplies to Russia. He had also diverted a proportion of his U boats from patrolling the Atlantic for the same reasons. While this alleviated the problem for Allied shipping on the Atlantic crossing it heralded great danger for the Arc tic convoys.

Convoy PQ12 set sail from Iceland on March 1st. The super German battleship Tirpitz, which always figured largely in Churchill's greatest fears, was ordered to intercept. Fortunately she was sighted by a British submarine and a combined fleet of the battleship King George V, the aircraft carrier Victorious, and various destroyers and smaller craft, moved on to the attack. PQ12 was not spotted by German aircraft so Tirpitz returned to Norway. PQ12 reached its destination safely with huge sighs of relief all round.

Three further convoys sailed for Russia in April and May of 1942. Heavy pack ice forced fourteen of the twenty three in the convoy to turn back. Nine ploughed on, only for one to be sunk by enemy action. Attacks by German aircraft, in particular, increased in ferocity when the next two convoys came in range. Ten ships, including the cruiser Edinburgh, were lost and fifty reached their destination with their precious cargo.

PQ 17 proved to be a disaster for the Allies. A convoy of thirty four merchant ships set sail from Iceland on June 27 bound for Archangel. A substantial escort, comprising six destroyers, two anti-aircraft ships, two submarines and eleven smaller craft sailed with it supported by four cruisers, and three destroyers, under Rear Admiral Hamilton. A screen of submarines was patrolling the north coast of Norway keeping a watchful eye on the German battleship "Tirpitz" and its supporting cruisers. Some distance to the west cruised the British battleship "Duke of York" and the American "Washington ", with the aircraft carrier "Victorious," three cruisers and a flotilla of destroyers, under the command of Admiral Tovey.

The convoy passed to the north of Bear Island in pack ice three hundred miles from German air bases and therefore well out of range. Rear Admiral Hamilton was ordered not to go any further. Tovey's force remained 150 miles north west of Bear Island ready for the "Tirpitz" to put in an appearance.

On July Ist came the first German attack with the first ship being sunk on July 4th. On the same day the Admiralty learned that the "Tirpitz" had sailed from Trondheim.The slow speed of the convoy, determined by the speed of the slowest ship. meant that seven or eight knots was all that could be achieved. "Tirpitz" would be among them in no time. The order came at 9.36 p.m. for the convoy to scatter. Unfortunately all escort vessels left the scene shortly afterwards. In reality the "Tirpitz" and its escorting destroyers did not leave their berths until midday on the 5th. The German commander feared an air attack but nevertheless continued on his mission until ordered by German High Command to return to base, leaving the attack on the convoy to aircraft and Uboats.

They wreaked havoc on the helpless merchant ships sinking twenty three. Only two British, six American, one Panamian and two Russian ships reached Archangel, delivering 70,000 tons out of the 200,000 which had left Iceland.

Churchill called for a pause in the shipping, citing a stockpile of goods but a shortage of ships. It was September before the next convoy sailed, escorted by sixteen destroyers and the aircraft carrier "Avenger" carrying twelve fighters. Attacks by enemy aircraft saw twenty

four of them shot down. Twelve merchant ships were lost but twenty seven arrived safely.

PQ19 sailed in December in two groups. The first suffered no losses. The second saw a battle between German pocket battleships "Lutzow" and heavy cruiser "Hipper" on the one hand and British cruisers "Sheffield" and "Jamaica", plus seven destroyers. The German admiral believed a formidable battle lay over the horizon so retired to port. Only one merchant ship suffered slight damage, all reaching safe Russian waters.

By the end of 1942, Arctic convoys had delivered 24,400 vehicles, 3,276 tanks, 2,665 aircraft, 514,664 tons of ammunition and 69,483 tons of oil and petroleum. The Russians were grateful, but still hoped for more.

At the end of February, 1942, Japanese forces captured Singapore.

CHAPTER THREE.

THE ROYAL NAVAL PATROL
SERVICE.

 Formed in 1940, the RNPS was an innovative
idea to provide a group of ships and sailors
which could "clear up" those irksome duties
which the RN deemed time consuming when
their attention was focussed on fighting the
enemy. In other words RNPS was the dogsbody
of the Navy. It did not even have a ship worthy
of the name, but, instead, any old hulk which
could be made to float again, or any fishing boat
which could be converted for use was soon
commandeered for service.

Informality was the key practice to be adopted
by those who served in RNPS. There was no
official uniform when they sailed out of port.
They only donned their uniform when they went
ashore. Flat caps, grey flannels, open neck shirts

and sea boots were commonly worn. For the most part, when at sea, men went unshaven. All in all, the crews of RNPS boats were, with complete justification, dubbed "Churchill's Pirates." Any RN officer, unlucky enough to meet these men, recoiled in horror.

Odd jobs were their metier. Transporting goods, stores and supplies was a common, almost daily, task. In a more exciting and demanding role, RNPS ships acted as minesweepers, which, in the early days, was a distinctly hazardous affair. Locating and identifying a mine was the first step. One crew had the mortifying experience of firing wildly at what was assumed to be a mine, only to discover, on closer inspection, that it was a dead horse.

The HQ was a large house in Lowestoft which the RN had named HMS Europa. This was quickly changed to the Sparrow's Nest when RNPS took over. One thing did please RNPS personnel – they were paid an extra 6 shillings a week for "roughing it." The official term was "Hard Lying" and was much to the disgust of serving sailors in the RN. The sole identification which RNPS ratings had was a silver badge on the sleeve.

Many of the seamen were fugitives from Nazi invasion. Fishermen from Denmark, Norway and the Netherlands sailed their fishing boats to Britain, rather than see them fall into the hands of the invader. The RNPS was an ideal home for them and they quickly adapted themselves to their new occupation. They were popular with their new friends and many a lasting bond was formed. Harold was no exception and quickly made friends with his new shipmates, most of whom were former fishermen. The skipper was a lieutenant in the RN and recognised that he had a fellow RN man who, in contrast with the rest of the Lowestoft complement, was always smartly turned out. Harold dismissed the chance to be a petty officer – "........an officer is only as good as the men he commands..." was his philosophy, and instead was appointed as leading steward. Meantime, he boarded with a series of landladies.

9 a.m. was "Fall-in." A P.A. system blared the various directions to the men on parade. Harold was told to take some on a route march around Lowestoft. They set off smartly but, once out of sight of the barracks, they relaxed and even had a quiet smoke, all under Harold's supervision, before returning in parade order.

Harold was told to go to the officers' mess which was housed in a beautiful seaside mansion, and wait for the telephone to ring, at which time he would take all messages and report them to the C.O. Twelve Wrens were in charge of all cooking and cleaning in the mansion. AT 6 a.m. Harold made them each a cup of tea and served it to them in bed. All strictly against the rules, of course!

From there it was back to the more serious business of getting back to war. Harold attended gunnery courses and learned how to strip down a Hotchkiss machine gun, which were found on most of the ships to be used by the RNPS.

The armament provided on board was unfamiliar to most of the seamen. Practice was required urgently and men were eager to get to grips with the guns provided. Many of the boats also carried depth charges, another novelty requiring more practice, with the added bonus that crews were able to supplement their rations with the dead fish which resulted from the explosions.

Seydisfjördur

CHAPTER FOUR.

PQ13.

PQ 13 was the first of three Arctic convoys in which Harold sailed. Had it not been for the unusual ailment anhidrosis, the inability to sweat, which meant that sailing in warm climates would have seen him in sick bays sooner than later, in all probability he would never seen service in the far north. As it was he was about to endure the worst sea journey in the world. He was issued with a chit to collect his suitable clothing. The clothing he received fell short of what a normal RN sailor would have expected which was a fur lined duffel coat, two pairs of woollen long johns, a white polo necked jersey, thick mittens and sea boot socks. The clothing Harold received was a balaclava, a waterproof canvas coat, woollen mittens, sea boots and canvas gloves. Nevertheless Harold always got on with the job and accepted his duty without question. Not all of his shipmates felt the same sense of duty. On hearing of their destination several of them ran away. Harold stopped one from running away by locking him in a vegetable locker. When informed of his new posting, Harold set off for Barry in south Wales where he joined his new ship, a former whaler called Sumba. The Sumba sailed on to Penzance, suffering from a buffeting from the weather which caused her to be moored for a few days while repairs were carried out. Then it was on to Falmouth where she picked up three submarines to be dropped off in sequence at Milford Haven, Liverpool and finally Dunoon. From Dunoon she sailed over to Belfast before making her way to Loch Ewe, then across to Stornoway, before finally joining the convoy at Seidisfjord on the east coast of Iceland.

Throughout the war years, Harold and Beatrice exchanged letters every week. Harold's letters were vetted by a senior R.N. officer – the wartime warning , with which everyone was familiar, was "careless talk costs lives." The upshot was that Beatrice did not know where

Harold was off to whenever he joined a new ship,

Loch Ewe , a sea loch in Wester Ross in the north west Highlands of Scotland, was a carefully chosen assembly point for convoys, big enough to hold the entire British fleet. It was almost out of range of German aircraft based in Norway and was selected to confuse German intelligence.

The Sumba, in common with its sister whalers , Sulla and Silja, was destined be given to the Russians once the convoy had arrived safely. They were built by the Smiths Dock Company of South Dock on Tees, each of 251 tons displacement and launched on or about the 20th June 1929.They joined the Salvesen whaling fleet but in 1940 were commissioned by the Admiralty and transferred to Russia in February 1942. They were built up at the bow and raked down aft. Harold claimed that you could put your foot in the water. For armament she carried a two-pounder cannon up front, twin Lewis guns, one to either side of the bridge, and a 2.5

inch machine gun aft. Unfortunately the two pounder lost its barrel the first time it was fired. A double "L" sweep was attached to the hull to aid minesweeping. The Captain of Sumba was William Edward Peters R.N.R.

The assembled convoy comprised merchant ships from several different nations. The Tobruk was Polish, The Gallant Fox and the Raceland were Panamian, The El Estea, Ballot, Bateau and Mona were from Honduras, the Empire Ranger, Empire Cowper, Empire Starlight, Induna, Scottish American, Harpelion, Lars Kruse and the New Westminster City were British and the Effingham, Eldena, Marmacmar and Dunboyne were from USA. Commander of the convoy was D A Casey, R.N.R. sailing on the River Afton. The Scottish American was an escort oiler vessel.

The cruisers Trinidad, Edinburgh and Kent, destroyers Fury and Lamerton, trawlers Blackfly and Paynter, and finally whalers Sumba, Sulla and Silja provided close escort.

On the possibility that Tirpitz, Scharnhorst, Gneisenau and the rest of the German fleet could be lured from their Norwegian haven, the Royal Navy mustered battleships King George V, Duke of York, battle cruiser Renown, the aircraft carrier Victorious and eleven destroyers to patrol the area to the west of Bear Island.

The convoy sailed from Iceland on the 21st March. On the 23rd a storm sprang up. Visibility deteriorated because the spray that was generated by high winds soon turned to ice. In turn ice covered everything. It proved difficult to keep the convoy together and on course, instead ships were ordered to rendezvous south of Bear Island which proved impossible. By this time the convoy had effectively dispersed.

Harold takes up the story in his own words – "......................The three whalers Sumba, Silja and Sulla, left Seidisfjord on Sunday, 22nd March with orders to join the convoy at position X which was 68 degrees fifty minutes North and 70 degrees thirty minutes West. We joined the convoy in the afternoon. We were told to take up station on the port bow of the convoy by the Senior Officer of the close escort in HMS Fury. Silja and Sulla were to follow at the rear of the convoy. In the morning we were ordered to drop astern and the three whalers were lying abreast of each other. Then it started blowing a gale together with the thickest snow obscuring our vision. The ship was icing up very quickly and I spent my time lashed to the funnel chopping the ice away with an axe which was reforming as fast as I could try to get rid of it. The Sulla was having the same difficulties. I kept looking at her now and again. Then the last time I looked she had disappeared. I assumed that the weight of the ice had turned her over and she had sunk without a trace.......................I don't wish to recall that journey from Hell............" Harold knew many of the Sulla crew. Had it not been for the entirely unselfish attitude he adopted to the job in hand (..."I was only doing my duty...") in all probability Sumba herself would have capsized.

. Typically Harold understates the true "Hell" of
what he had to endure. Insufficiently dressed as
he was, he did not hesitate to volunteer to be the
one to go on deck and get rid of the ice as much
as possible. Although Sumba was a whaler,
designed to cope with rough seas, it is doubtful
if she had ever sailed in seas such as this. Waves
climbed to huge, unimaginable heights, and then
dropped the ship to the foot of the next
monstrous roller. The gale tossed the ship from
side to side at the same time. Trying to maintain
a foothold was an almost impossible task. It was
only by being lashed to the funnel that Harold
was prevented from being swept overboard into
an ocean which allowed the unfortunate
swimmer a mere two minutes to survive .Not
that Harold was still able to escape the waves
which burst over him every few seconds. Spume
and spray covered his eyebrows with ice. The
very hairs in his nostrils froze solid which meant
that breathing through the nose was an intensely
painful experience. Only by taking quick,
shallow breaths through the mouth could he
continue. In such conditions it is no surprise that

Harold was seasick all of the time aboard. He lived in the engineer's compartment to the aft of the ship, so he was tossed about more than the others whose berths were amidships.

Conditions below deck were not much better. The constant pounding of the sea soaked everything .The fire in the stove quickly went out. Everything which was not fastened firmly down was flung around the cabin and galley. Even the contents of the "heads" were splattered everywhere. When an exhausted Harold finally came below he sank into a bunk which was thoroughly soaked. There was no escape from Nature's fury. Harold was too shattered physically to care, but flopped down as he was, still fully clothed and not even bothering to remove his clothes.

There was no possibility of warm food, instead corned beef in wet bread was all there was to eat and kye (cocoa) to drink. For the duration of the entire voyage, Harold did not see any officers who were probably happy to stay in the wheelhouse or anywhere free of the storm.

Captain Peters swung his craft north in a bid to escape the worst of the weather. Unfortunately Sumba sailed into an ice pack and was soon unable to move. It must have seemed to Harold that this was it. There was soon an end to available food, such as it was. Fuel, too, was nearly all gone. Captain Peters ordered help to be radioed in the hope someone would hear. The plea was picked up by the destroyer Fury which was engaged in rounding up stragglers and directing them to the convoy position. Sumba was fifty miles north of Bear Island when Fury found her. An anxious four and threequarter hours followed while refuelling took place. A load of bread loaves was dropped on Sumba's deck, quickly seized by a starving crew. Harold had been reduced to scraping green mould from a rasher of bacon before chewing it. The Captain of Fury was not pleased that Sumba had broken radio silence, thus placing his own ship, as well as Sumba, in great peril of attack. Once a passage in the ice had been cleared by a Russian ice breaker, Sumba sailed on.

Elsewhere in the convoy further trouble was brewing. Induna came under attack by a German aircraft but managed to fight it off. Slowly the ships came to form line ahead and struggled on in groups at a maximum of nine knots.

On the 28th March the weather improved. A clear, sunny day meant for swifter progress but also increased the likelihood of German attacks. Trinidad fired at a Blohm and Voss BV138 reconnaissance seaplane which cheekily flashed back " Your shots are falling short." It was possibly the same aircraft which swept down on the unprotected Harold as he remained fastened to the Sumba funnel. In a horrid fascination he watched as the machine gun bullets traced a path across the deck, missing his feet by no more than a foot. At this stage the convoy was only 150 miles from the Banak aircraft base in North Norway which meant more attacks were inevitable. Three German destroyers sailed from Kirkenes in Norway to intercept the convoy. Soon the trawler Paynter was attacked from the air and the Silja and Blackfly were bombed by a

Junkers 88 bomber. The air attack was now in full swing. Trinidad was fired at from the air, while Raceland and Empire Ranger were sunk by bombs. Next to go was Bateau which was sunk by gunfire from a German destroyer.

Just in time help arrived in the form of two Russian destroyers, Sokrushitelni and Gremyash chi. Trinidad now found herself attacked by two German destroyers but managed to avoid the torpedoes they fired at her. In return she fired a torpedo at an attacker only to find that, by some freak accident, the torpedo described a circle and turned back towards the helpless Trinidad, striking her amidships in the Royal Marines' quarters killing many of them instantly and wounding many more. It is believed that the gyroscope on the torpedo, which controls the steering, had frozen solid and was therefore unable to respond properly. The German destroyer Z26, which had therefore had a lucky escape, did not escape the shelling from Eclipse, a British destroyer. Six hits sent the foe to the bottom.

More help arrived from the Kola base in the form of minesweepers Horner, Gossamer, Hussar and Speedwell to act as escort. The hapless Trinidad limped into Kola . Finally Effingham was torpedoed by a Uboat and sank, which fate also befell Induna. In the latter case survivors took to the lifeboats and underwent an ordeal lasting four days before a Russian minesweeper found them. Meanwhile Silja, the sister ship to Sumba, made it to port safely, having saved a sole survivor of a sunken merchant vessel, who was found floating aimlessly in a lifeboat.

At long last, after an ordeal of ten days, most of the convoy, including Sumba, reached safety. Sumba docked at Polyarnoe, the Soviet Northern Fleet Headquarters, near the entrance to the Kola inlet. Harold and his shipmates stepped ashore to a hero's welcome. Even though it was a pitch black evening, A Captain from a Russian merchant vessel took Harold to his ship and introduced him to the crew, many of whom were female. Harold passed a wonderful night asleep on a bunk which did not move at all, with sheet, blankets and pillow which were dry! The next morning Harold had an important visitor, Admiral Golovko whose first words (in impeccable English) were "...it's a bloody miracle that you got that ship here." Golovko was destined to play a leading role in Russian participation in the Arctic convoys . He was described by Rear Admiral Burrough RN as "....clever, far-seeing and probably ruthless....possessing the ability to weigh up a situation very rapidly, but definitely a man of the people. A rough diamond, quite unpolished and with poorish table manners. Rather scruffy but surprisingly well read. Very keen to cooperate and undoubtedly a capable man .I found him likeable, friendly and frank."

On a table nearby was a set of Chinese checkers, so the Admiral challenged Harold to a game which the former won. Harold went ashore to see the sights such as they were. He noticed a queue of Russian sailors outside a hairdresser's. When Harold was spotted he was taken straight to the head of the queue. Women barbers attended to him once inside.

Harold was given accommodation in the Russian Naval barracks where a meal of stewed reindeer was waiting. One of Harold's shipmates turned up his nose at the meal so Harold said "I'll have yours as well." It was while dining that Harold saw the officers from the Sumba, the first time he had seen them since leaving Iceland!

A Board of Enquiry was assembled on board HMS Harrier at Polyarnoe to enquire into the loss at sea of HMS whaler Sulla on passage from Iceland to the Kola Inlet. Summing up, the Enquiry Board wrote in their report "...Sulla was last seen at dark on 24th March 1942 in the station astern of the convoy in approximate position 70 degrees and 15 minutes North, 2 degrees and 10 minutes East. The cause of the loss cannot be stated definitely. In our opinion the most probable cause of her loss would appear to be capsizing owing to the weight of ice in weather conditions which made it extremely difficult to remove the ice. From Sumba's evidence the icing conditions on the night Sulla was lost were severe." Harold, who was probably the only eye witness to the dreadful event, was not called to the Enquiry.

Harold was given a pass which allowed him to roam freely throughout the Polyarnoe base which lasted for three weeks. A Russian sailor took Harold to Rosta further up the Kola inlet. There he watched as the Trinidad finally made harbour and docked, to unload the bodies of those marines killed by torpedo explosion, as well as the many who were severely injured. It was a pitiful sight.

Harold sailed home on the cruiser Liverpool from Murmansk which was attacked by German destroyers but drove them off. The ship finally reached Stromness sometime in early May. There was no one to meet it. From there Harold made his way to Scrabster, Thurso and Ardrossan where he reported to the R.N. headquarters. He was given a travel warrant to Lowestoft. When he arrived he was greeted with "Where the bloody hell have you been?"

Harold O'Neill RN

Sumba shipmates.

CHAPTER FIVE.

MORE SUPPLIES TO RUSSIA.

Although Harold sailed in two further Arctic convoys, he remembers nothing about them at all. It is more than likely that his brain shut down its own defence mechanism to prevent any further occurrence of the dreadful experiences he suffered on PQ13.

The medical term for this condition is "psychogenic amnesia" or "disassociative amnesia." It is defined as a memory disorder characterized by sudden retrograde autobiographical memory loss said to occur for a period of time ranging from hours to years – an inability to recall personal information usually of a traumatic or stressful nature e.g. child abuse or soldiers returning from combat.

Existing records of crew lists show that Harold sailed on convoy JW 52 which left Liverpool on 7th January, 1943 and arrived at the Kola Inlet on the 27th January 1943, then the RA53 convoy which left the Kola Inlet on the 1st March, 1943 and arrived at Loch Ewe on the 14th of March. There were four merchant ships from USA, nine from Uk and one Panamanian. The escort was provided by corvettes Lotus and Starwort, the minesweeper Britannia and trawlers Northern Pride (Harold's ship), and St. Elstan. Destroyers Onslaught, Offa, Matchless, Mushota, Beagle, Bulldog and Piorun provided what was called the "ocean escort," while cruisers Kent, Bermuda and Glasgow sailed from Bear Island to Kola inlet. The Northern pride was, in fact, a former German fishing vessel which had been converted to an escort vessel.

The weather stayed fine and the convoy made good progress. Air attacks did take place on the 24th January, from four He115 torpedo bombers, but two were shot down and the others bid a hasty retreat.

Eventually the convoy reached its destination on the 27th January.

Harold stayed with the Russians and their heartfelt hospitality until March 1st when Commander Malcolm Goldsmith took RA 53 out of the Kola inlet and headed for home. There were thirty westbound merchantmen in the convoy, protected by the cruiser Scylla, thirteen destroyers, corvettes Poppy, Starwort, Lotus and Bergamot, and the trawlers St. Elstan and Northern Pride which was Harold's ship. The convoy was soon spotted by a patrolling Uboat which trailed it for three days, looking for an opportunity to launch an attack.. Meanwhile a dozen Junkers 88s had no success in trying to bomb the convoy, being driven off by an effective barrage put up from the escort and the merchantmen. A torpedo did sink the Executive and two "Liberty" ships (supplied by the USA), which had been welded quickly to make them available as soon as possible, began to founder when their welds split in the heavy seas. One was taken under tow by HMS Opportune and all the way to Iceland, a considerable feat of seamanship.

Puerto Rican was also sunk by torpedo and all of her crew were lost. The Richard Bland was blown in two by a torpedo.

Harold and the Northern Pride finally arrived at Loch Ewe on the 14th March. From the 7th January to 14th March , Harold was away from the UK for some 63 days. He has no recollection of even the slightest event during all of that time.

In total, 78 convoys sailed to Russia to provide vital arms and ammunition in the dreadful war against the Nazi invader. The last convoy sailed from Scotland on May 12th, 1945 and arrived at the Kola Inlet on May 20th. By that time, the war in Europe was, to all intents and purposes, over and the Allies had totally destroyed their German opponents. In point of fact, the war had turned against Hitler's men by the end of 1942, although the desperate struggle continued for a further three years. It can be seen, therefore, that the 1942 convoys and the cargo they carried , were the crucial ones that enabled the Russians to carry on the fight. Thereafter, Russian factories in the vast hinterland lying to the east of Moscow were rapidly pouring out vast amounts of their own armaments, especially the T34 tank which virtually won the war on its own at the Battle of Kursk.

Altogether 581 merchant ships took part in the convoys. Of these 292 were American, 184 were British, 56 Russian, 29 Panamanian, 11 Norwegian, 5 Dutch, 2 were from Honduras and one each from Belgium and Denmark. They carried aircraft, tanks, jeeps, lorries, bicycles, anti-aircraft guns, sub-machine guns (or "tommy-guns"), tons of explosives, locomotives, railway wagons, steel rails, miles and miles of telephone cable, food, petrol, tyres, chemicals, leather and 15 million pairs of boots – all to feed the Russian war machine. The human cost to the Allies was 829 lives in87 merchant ships, while 1,944 men died in 18 men-of-war.

Harold returned to RNPS duties which saw him take on a number of roles and serve first on the Strathgarry, a gunnery fire-ship. The ship was used to train gunners for the RN. Harold served as a Leading Officers' Steward and also helped to clean the wounds of a gunner who was hurt when the battery of an Oerlikon anti –gun exploded.

Beatrice waited at home for news of her boyfriend. Letters came spasmodically and had been scrutinised carefully beforehand by RN security officers, so that she was totally unaware of the perils of sailing on Arctic convoys never mind the less demanding duties that Harold had undertaken in his various roles with the RNPS. She longed for the day when her handsome sailor boy would come striding down the street. Her wartime work in the factories kept her mind focussed during the day but she always hurried home to see if any letter was waiting for her. When it was her lucky day she read the contents over and over again and was deliriously happy - at least for a short while. The days and months crawled by and it seemed to her that the war would never end. Infrequent leaves spelt bliss while they lasted but always ended too quickly. Like thousands of other couples up and down the country happiness was put on hold. Reports of naval engagements, wherever they occurred, filled her with alarm until word arrived that Harold was not involved.

At last the great news. Harold was given sufficient leave to enable them to get married. The ceremony took place at St Andrews church on March 18th 1944. The courtship had lasted four years. There were no wedding photographs due to because of a prior engagement. Cameras were not to be found during the war years so no one in the congregation could step into the breach. After the wedding Harold took his new bride with him to York where they stayed with a Mts Blackburn, a friend's mother.Then it was back to Norwich where they stayed at a hotel. Beatrice was working twelve hours a day in artificial light. Harold was increasingly concerned at the effect on her general health. He managed to secure her release and they moved to Suffolk to Bungay which sat on the edge of a fifteen mile restricted military zone. They found lodgings with Mrs Honeywood from where Harold cycled fifteen miles every day to his work. They eventually found a house at Lowestoft. They were fortunate to find a house available for purchase, mainly because it was reputed to be haunted by an old man who sat in a chair by the fireside. Harold said he hoped he did not mind him sitting on top of him!. The next stop was Queenborough, on the Isle of Sheppey, where Harold was posted. Beatrice returned home to Stanley where her mother could look after her. Harold was involved in minesweeping duties on a "four days out, four days in" basis. The main area to be swept clear of mines was off the Scheldt islands in the North Sea. Harold was able to return to his wife's side for Christmas 1944 took over the cooking of the dinner for all of the family.

Harold also served on HMS Carrick which was a converted sailing ship, used as a hotel for those in transit from ship to ship. The ship was moored at Port Glasgow and Harold was there for one week before sailing from the Broomielaw to Belfast and HMS Caroline, a refitted cruiser which had fought Jutland in WW1. While serving on the Caroline, Harold helped to lift a racing cutter out of the water, then clean it of barnacles before giving it a new coat of paint. The cutter took part in a race against a crew from another ship. Harold acted as stroke and won the race. Then it was back to canteen duties. The canteen was manned by volunteers, Harold included, but on one occasion, the Marchioness of Dufferin and Ava, no less, decided to help with the washing up. Harold said "You dry and I'll wash." An Irish pal took Harold to a farm on the Mountains of Mourne for a break.

When Harold returned to the Belfast office a message was waiting which instructed him to return to Lowestoft as a priority. From Lowestoft he was told to go to Southampton to find the " River Leven" and await instructions. Southampton was crowded with troops, both American and British, army vehicles of all types including hundreds of tanks , ships and landing craft by the hundred – but no "River Leven." Enquiries at the RN reception HQ revealed that no one had ever heard of it. Harold was told to call again next day. He found a hotel and stayed there for a week while he sought the elusive ship. With nothing to do Harold visited Winchester and surrounding places of interest while Allied forces took part in the biggest invasion by sea ever. Eventually Harold did find the "River Leven." It had been involved in the landings in Normandy.

On board at last Harold took on duties as a mess steward to the officers as well as helping out as cook on alternate days since the appointed individual, who should have worked full time in the galley, had little or no idea how to cook or even where to find the necessary food. Harold discovered some "K" rations, originally intended for US troops, commandeered them and used them for meals. Another good deed was to find extra blankets for the crew. Of course, this resulted in good food and warmth all round. He even volunteered as a stoker to relieve other stokers and keep the boat going. Perhaps it was in performing this task that Harold contracted a painful ear cyst. At the time the ship was tied up on the Clyde so Harold went to the Greenock Hospital and then to the Royal Canadian Hospital on HMS Niobe. This took place in the week before Christmas and Harold asked to stay in the hospital rather than going back to his ship, knowing full well the state the crew would be in. On Boxing Day he did return to find the whole crew unconscious following Yuletide celebrations.

The "River Leven," having been deemed to have completed its wartime service, was returned to its owners at Percy Main on the Tyne in Northumberland. Harold sailed with her. When leave had ended Harold hitched a lift on a tank landing craft sailing from Tilbury to Ostend where he joined MMS 265, a mine sweeper made of wood. It carried a big drum on the stern which itself carried two cables, each five inches thick, lashed together. The final thirty yards of the cable composed a copper wire. A battery was housed in a compartment beneath the cable. When trailed over the stern of the ship and the battery was switched on, an electrical input created a magnetic field. When detonated in this way some explosions lifted the rear of the ship clear out of the water. Some floating mines were shot at with rifles which was not an easy task given a constantly moving target and only a small projection to aim at.

MMS265 joined a fleet of 200 minesweepers combing the North Sea off Antwerp for mines. This was the largest minesweeping patrol ever assembled but size alone did not guarantee safety in what was always a hazardous occupation. To bring home the point spectacularly, the minesweeper sailing behind MMS265 in line blew up.

Harold resumes the next part of his story in his own words –"...I was serving on MMS265 tied up to the jetty after doing our normal sweeping of the approaches to the Thames, when all ships companies were told to fall in on the jetty to be addressed by Captain M/S.

Captain Hopper RN informed us that the war in Europe had ended and that we were all free to go up to London to join in the celebrations, with the proviso that we had to be back on board our respective ships by the last train as we were sailing early in the morning for the Hook of Holland.

We were fallen out and I lost no time in collecting my wife who was living in Queensborough at the time. We went to the station and some of the lads had already started celebrating, hosing each other down with the fire hose on the station platform. We caught our train and arrived at London Bridge station and were caught up in the immense crowds in the Capital. The feeling was electric . Everyone was so relieved that after all this time the war was over. No one seemed to care that Japan had still to be dealt with. People were dancing and singing , all nationalities whatever their colour, race or creed were joining in this expression of happiness and relief. We were all happy to be alive.

My wife and I tried to get up Shaftesbury Avenue but the American band was playing on the balcony of the Rainbow Club and the crowd made it impossible to move. We were all trying to dance shoulder to shoulder. We eventually made it to the Queen Victoria Monument in front of Buckingham Palace. There were people everywhere in front of the Palace and the Mall was jammed all the way up to Admiralty Arch. One thing I remember was a Jewish gentleman on the steps below us jumping up and down shouting "Ve vant the King, ve vant the King." His enthusiasm knew no bounds and when the Royal Family appeared on the Palace balcony with Winston Churchill the crowd cheered themselves hoarse. What a day to remember! The next day we were in Holland tied up at the Hook and the place was alive with members of the German army sitting playing cards in the sun."

Harold had served in the RN for most of the war years, but it was not quite all over for him. There was still an enormous amount of clearing up to be done. The seas around Great Britain were brimming with mines which had been laid by both the Allies and Germans. A resumption of normal, peacetime merchant activities would be hazardous until every one of these dangerous devices was blown up. It was down to Harold and his minesweeper shipmates to see the task completed.

Wedding day for Beatrice and Harold.

CHAPTER SIX

POST WAR IN CIVVY STREET.

Harold spent the rest of 1945 on MMS 265, clearing mines from the North Sea. At one stage he and a shipmate landed on the Dutch shore and commandeered a German officer's Peugeot car. They drove to the Hague and went sightseeing. Harold bought a coffee set for twenty five guilders which is still in his possession. Back on board, MMs 265 helped to clear the Maas river, Leyden and the Amsterdam ship canal. On another trip to Amsterdam, following a lift by a Dutch fire engine crew, a shopkeeper gave him a brush down and a little girl tried to present him with a posy of flowers. Instead Harold bought the whole bunch and told her to take them home to her mother.

He was finally discharged in early 1946 having spent six years with the Royal Navy. Great Britain had endured the ravages of war for longer than any of the other involved nations.

Coming on top of the first World War, she had seen ten years of the first half of the twentieth century given to fighting in all corners of the earth. She was an exhausted country, with an economy which was barely managing to feed her people, heavily in debt and with a manpower seriously depleted. This was the picture facing Harold and thousands of other men on their return from foreign parts.

He was now, of course, a married man and also a father since Beatrice had given birth to a bouncing baby boy on the twentieth of October 1945. He was named David and a source of pure delight to his ecstatic parents. Harold had to find a job quickly. His first call was to the Labour Exchange at Stanley, County Durham. This led him to take a bricklaying course at Felling on Tyne which lasted for six months. It was not to Harold's liking so he was relieved when the opportunity arose to join Hadrian's the Grocers, following an advertisement in the local press. He was taken on a one month's trial at the Consett branch. There was an exceptionally heavy fall of snow that winter and, on one occasion, the bus which was taking Harold to work was stuck, unable to move either forwards or backwards. Nothing daunted, Harold climbed out and began to walk inasmuch as he was able to do so. At one stage he found the snow was so deep that he was walking over two submerged buses which had also become victims of the atrocious weather. Eventually Harold reached the store where he was working only to find the roof had collapsed. There was no work that day!

The newlyweds were living with Beatrice's parents until a new estate of council houses opened for rent, whereupon they rented a new home in Hollyhill Gardens East. Harold changed jobs to become a shopworker with Blackhill Fruiterers. He spent the first three weeks of his employment killing rats including one occasion where he found they had even invaded the supposedly secure potato locker. A better wage was found when he moved to Ransom and Marles ball-bearing factory at Greencroft, which had rapidly switched from wartime production to supplying motoring firms. Harold was a machinist, and then a setter-operator which required him to work to tolerances of two-thousandth of an inch. As a leader of men in the wartime years, he was a natural choice to become the union representative. His wartime experience had, unfortunately, affected his health and he sustained an attack of dermatitis. It was clear that the factory atmosphere did not suit him. Off duty he was asked, by the police, to be a second at a boxing tournament and thoroughly enjoyed the experience. He left his job at Ransom and Marles in 1947 and instead became a grocer again, this time at the Burnopfield Co-Operative Store in Rowlands Gill.

His old life at sea still held an attraction for him, and led to him joining the RNVR at Newcastle as a steward as he had been previously during the war. This was only a part-time appointment but he took full advantage of his new position. He even contrived to sleep in the Commander's cabin! Back home after being reviewed by Her Majesty during a "celebrations" parade in

London, he took driving lessons in Newcastle and passed first time. This enabled him to take over the Co-Op travelling shop on its daily journey through the highways and byways of County Durham. The family was growing in number with the arrival of Ann on the second of June 1949 and Pamela on the second of March 1952. With some regret Harold was obliged to quit his job with the Co-op and seek more remunerative employment. His new position was in the Planning Department of Ransom, Hoffmann and Pollard, formerly Ransom and Marles. There he was involved with the first computer installation which took place at Ferrybridge.

A growing family placed increasing pressure on the income, and Harold was continually on the lookout for a better-paid position. This search took him to Appleyards at Leeds, a motor retailer, where he became an accounts clerk. All the time he was building up a useful supply of financial knowledge which soon came to the ears of Price, Waterhouse and Cooper. He was "headhunted" by them and invited to assist in winding up a company which had fallen on hard times. From there it was a swift move to stocktaking, again for Price, Waterhouse etc. They were very pleased with his work and his growing reputation for accuracy and hard work secured him a post as the Materials Controller which he worked at until he was asked to take on the headship of the sales department of Smith's Electric Vehicles on the Team Valley Estate, Gateshead. From there it was an easy commute to his family at home in Stanley. Orders were soon pouring in from all over the world, including an export trade with South Africa, notwithstanding Harold controlled six representatives in various areas of the United Kingdom.

There is little doubt that he would have continued with his job at Smiths had not fate intervened. The highly publicised new injection against influenza, the "flu jab," caused Harold to develop a severe reaction which left him completely listless and barely able to crawl around the house or even to the bathroom. He was confined to his bed for a total of twelve weeks and felt it was only fair to tell Smiths that he did not know when he would recover and that therefore he must resign. An advertisement in the Stanley News seeking applicants for the Planning Department at "Ransom and Marles, his old employer, stipulated an age limit of 35. Harold's standing with his old workmates was still high so he was given the job and, indeed, stayed there until 23/8/1977.

When daughter Pamela accepted a teaching post at a North Berwick primary school her parents decided to travel north with her. Harold was interviewed at Haddington labour Exchange and took a job as caretaker-gardener at Gourlaybank, looking after the gardens of forty houses. He helped to erect a marquee on the estate lawn as part of the celebrations of the Charles/Diana wedding in 1981 before finally retiring altogether in 1983. His family had all settled into their various careers. David, after several jobs, had become the Senior Communications Officer for the Fire Service for the whole of County Durham. Ann served customers behind the till at Marks and Spencer's prime store in Northumberland Street, Newcastle., while Pamela , as indicated above, followed a teaching career which took her from Delves Primary School, Consett to North Berwick.

Beatrice developed into a highly promising artist, mainly in watercolours, and many of her pictures adorn the lounge wall at Harold's current address in Haddington. The couple reached the outstanding milestone of sixty years married, which they celebrated at a David's house in Castleside, County Durham. Sadly, shortly after the event, Beatrice died in 2004.

CHAPTER SEVEN

CHEERS AND CHILL.

Recognition for the part played by those who sailed on the Arctic convoys took on a very different aspect in Russia and Great Britain. Harold describes his reception at Polyarnoe, following his epic voyage as part of convoyPQ13, as "outstanding." Men and women cheered and embraced him on every occasion he showed his face. Valuable and essential supplies of war weapons and materials were just what the doctor ordered, as far as the Russians were concerned. Their appreciation of the ordeal endured by men of the arctic convoys knew no bounds. Every man who sailed from UK to Russia was a hero in their eyes and would never be forgotten. Harold confirms this fact by his frequent attendance at the surprisingly large number of celebrations to which he has been invited over the years, culminating in the 70th commemoration of the end of the "Great Patriotic War," as the Russians term it, which was held in St. Petersburg in the summer 0f 2015. Harold was escorted by his son, David, throughout the trip. No expense was spared by their hosts. They stayed at the best hotels, ate food fit for a king, were entertained by a wide variety of events, and even given flowers by the children who were part of the 158,000 crowd watching the parade of Russian military might. A special cheer was accorded Harold and other veterans of the Arctic convoys who were part of the parade. Father and son will never forget it. Altogether Harold had already received two medals from Russia for Arctic Service, plus three anniversary medals. A citation for the Jubilee medal reads as follows : "Harold O'Neill. By order of the President of the Russian Federation on 4th March 2009 is awarded the Jubilee medal on the 65th anniversary of victory in the Great Patriotic War 1941-45. On behalf of the President of the Russian Federation the medal was presented on 23 April 2010 by the Consul General of Russia in Edinburgh." The supreme Russian medal was awarded him on the 24th of June 2013. This was the Ushakov medal, named after a famed Russian hero, 1745- 1817, an admiral in the Russian navy at the time of Nelson. Ushakov fought 43 battles at sea and never lost either a battle or a ship. This award is the highest given in Russia. The citation reads "It is a pleasure and an honour to write to you on the very prominent and long- awaited occasion of the award of the Ushakov medal to the Scottish veterans of the Arctic convoys and recognition of your bravery and contribution to the cause of defeating Nazism during the Second World War." – Andrei Pritsepov, Russian Consul General.

Although the Arctic convoys were mentioned in the wartime press and featured in the Pathe news on cinema screens throughout Great Britain, there was no corresponding outburst of congratulation for the crews of the ships which had sailed to Russia to deliver desperately needed arms and supplies. In 1946 the Campaign medal, 1939-45, a war service medal for which the qualifying period of service was 28 days at sea, was awarded to Harold. There followed the

Atlantic Star,1939-45, plus bar which
represented France and Germany, the Naval
General Service medal ,first instituted in 1847,
plus minesweeping clasp, and two
Commemorative medals for a) service in the
Arctic and b) service in the Royal Naval Patrol
service. Many of Harold's Russian medals are
made of gold. The end of the war had seen the
Russians extend their powers of influence far to
the west, to such an extent that the Western
powers were afraid of just how far the Russians
would go. Churchill expressed these fears when
he pronounced an "Iron Curtain" had fallen
across Europe from the Arctic to the
Mediterranean. The western press lost no time in
enlarging on this situation, and any mention or
dealings with Russia were not to be
contemplated in the eyes of the public. Harold's
efforts, and those of his teammates, were quietly
filed away.

The situation might never have been resolved
had it not been for the unstinting work of
Commander William Grenfell RN, 1920-2013.

He himself had sailed on PQ16 to Murmansk on the Empire Lawrence which was dive-bombed and sank. He was thrown into the sea but was rescued and spent six months in a Russian Hospital before being repatriated to UK. He had been promised a medal for bravery shown during the attack but it never materialised. In 1980 he joined the Russian Convoy Club in Portsmouth and in 1985 was persuaded to lead a campaign asking the Government to create a medal for the survivors of the Arctic convoys. Quite justifiably these men felt aggrieved that they were not eligible for a medal specifically awarded for their part in the Battle of the Atlantic, described by Winston Churchill as "the worst journey in the world." Contemporary politics, which shunned relationships with the Eastern bloc, would not hear of it. Even when an offer was on the table for award of the Ushakov medal it was denied. The Government argument was that King George V had said that medals should not be awarded for events which had taken place more than five years ago. Loud replies claimed that this was nonsense and posted examples in Malaya, Burma etc.. to show that medals had indeed been awarded outside the time frame named.

In desperation Grenfell stood for Parliament in order to draw attention to his campaign. He lost heavily but his efforts ensured that his name and cause were published in the daily papers. The Government of the day was caught in a dilemma. In 2006 in an effort to diffuse the situation they offered an Arctic Emblem lapel badge – "something you find at the bottom of a cornflakes packet" was Grenfell's scornful response. His struggle for recognition had not gone unnoticed in Moscow. In May 2010, he was invited to attend the Moscow Victory parade, followed by lunch at the Kremlin.

At last the British Government gave way. In December 2012 they announced the award of the Arctic Star medal to survivors of the Arctic convoys. Grenfell was the first to receive it. Sadly he died the following year. In June 2013 the Ushakov medal, which is made of silver, was awarded to the same survivors during President Putin's visit.

Harold wears his medals proudly. As one of the few survivors of World War Two, he leads the Remembrance Day Parade in Haddington and lays a wreath on the War Memorial. The sound of crashing breakers and the sight of ice forming all around him on the good ship Sumba, no doubt comes to him as he does so.

CONCLUSION.

Throughout a long life, Harold has remained true to himself and the standards he inherited from his parents. At no time could he ever be accused of cheating, lying or devious behaviour. He stood his ground when challenged, even when he risked rebuke, at the very least, from a superior officer. A typical example arose when his CO at Lowestoft ordered Harold to be issued with a white uniform, thereby indicating that Harold was going to sea somewhere where the weather was likely to be on the warm side. Given Harold's medical condition, i.e. anhidrosis, this could have proved fatal. His initial protest met with the usual reply, that he had to obey orders, but Harold would not be intimidated and told his CO of his problem. When offered the alternative of sailing on the Arctic convoy he did not hesitate to accept.

Harold invariably did his duty when others were all to ready to seek any escape. Again an obvious example was when Harold, alone, cleared from the deck of the Sumba. Had he not done so it may well have suffered the same fate as its sister ship, the Sulla, which capsized because of the weight of the ice it was carrying.

This is not to try to show Harold in too fine a light. He was quite capable of helping shipmates in situations when RN regulations were likely to be breached. Taking over stoker duties, which he was not qualified to do, so that the stoker in question could pay a quick home visit, was an example. On other occasions he turned a Nelsonian "blind-eye" to seamen antics. If Harold thought that he could help he usually was not found reluctant to do so.

Good health was a major factor in Harold's progress in the war years and later. At sea he had the odd cold, a cyst proved troublesome and his accident in ripping open his arm on the Northern pride nearly cost him dearly, but. Otherwise, he was able to go about his duties untroubled. In a way his anhidrosis proved to be a blessing. After boarding the LLanstephan Castle at Gourock to take him to Iceland he remembers nothing until he has returned to Lowestoft. This loss of memory allowed him to remember nothing of the other two Arctic convoys he sailed on. His smartly dressed appearance, especially, undoubtedly led to him being chosen to be steward on several occasions. His air of quiet authority led him to be put in charge of his peers and offered examples of his sympathetic style of leadership, although he always made sure the job was done properly whatever it was. He always believed in leading by example, and was the more respected for it.

His motivation came, no doubt, from thoughts of Beatrice and their future. No other girl was allowed to distract him. Their marriage was the fulfilment of all those days and nights alone on watch or carrying out some tedious chore. Sixty happy years together and a loving family was his reward to sticking to his guns and his personal beliefs.

Harold took everything in his stride and concentrated on the job in hand whatever it was.

He believed in, and gave, service to his employer, his country, his shipmates and his wife and family and did it all in his own relaxed style.

With the passage of time, it is still unclear what, precisely, was the Government's reason, or reasons for delaying the award of medals to those who sailed to Russia. Had no one sailed and carried arms etc. to Russia, then the outcome of World War Two would have been very different. It is likely that Nazi Germany would have taken Moscow and Russia would have sought peace terms, in which case Hitler could have focussed his entire military might on the conquest of Great Britain. The Cold War argument pales against the facts. Churchill called it "the worst journey in the world." Perhaps if he had retained power for longer following the end of the war he might have come round to doing something about it.

Thankfully, what was a great wrong has now been put right, and Harold and his surviving shipmates from the Arctic convoys can display their Arctic Star and other decorations with considerable pride.

THE END

NOTES.

Chapter One.

Nervo & Knox, who began their entertainment career as an acrobatic dancing duo, were part of the original Crazy Gang which performed on the stage of the Palladium during the 1940s.

Flanagan and Allen were also part of the Crazy Gang but became hugely popular with the British public with their comedy and especially their songs. Their most famous song, among hundreds, was "Underneath the Arches." Their song "Who do you think you are kidding, Mr Hitler?" still introduces the evergreen TV programme "Dad's Army."

Ivor Novello was born in Wales and became a composer and actor. His most famous song of the First World War was "Keep the Home Fires Burning." In the inter war period he wrote several stage musicals including "Glamorous

Night," "Dancing Years," and "Perchance to Dream."

Jack Buchanan portrayed the Mayfair man-about-town to perfection, although he was born in Helensburgh in Scotland. Always immaculately dressed he strolled about the stage as an actor, singer and dancer. One of his best known songs was "Goodnight Vienna." He had a long career in show business and in the film industry. In later years he became a producer and director.

Layton and Johnson were an American vocal and piano duet who became a feature of BBC radio broadcasts in the thirties, forties and early fifties. They sold over ten million records.

German battleships in WW2.

Tirpitz. – launched in 1941. The heaviest battleship ever built by a European navy. Armed with 8 X 38cm (15 inch) guns. Sailed to Norway to act as a deterrent to Arctic convoys. Damaged by British submarines and frequently attacked from the air. On the 12th November 1944

Lancaster bombers dropped bombs weighing 12,000 pounds, scoring two hits. The Tirpitz capsized and 1000 perished.

Scharnhorst. - a battleship launched in 1936. Armed with 9 X 28cm (11 inch) guns. Sank HMS Rawalpindi, a cruiser. Took part in the invasion of Norway. Sank aircraft carrier Glorious and destroyers Acasta and Ardent. Sailed up the Channel to Germany in 1943. Sank by HMS Duke of York during the battle of Gdynia in N.E. Poland.

Gneisenau – sister ship to the Scharnhorst. Launched in 1936. Bombed by British aircraft in 1942 and put out of action. Sunk as a blockship in Gdynia, N.E.Poland.

INDEX

Beamish St.	11
Bear Island	20, 31, 35, 43, 47
Beatrice	11,12, 50,52,60, 66,76
Belfast	28,50
Blackhill	61
Blohm and Voss	36
Borneo	72
Broomielaw	50
Buchanan, Jack	7
Buckingham Palace	56
Bungay	49
Burnhope	62
Burroughs	35
Busty Pit	2

P

St. Petersburg	68
Stornoway	28
Stratford on Avon	10
Stromness	41

SHIPS.

Allied Merchant Vessels

S.S.Ballot	30
" Bateau	30,37
" Blackburn	30,36
" Britannia	43
" Dunboyne	30
" Eldena	30
" Effingham	30,38
" El Estea	30
" Empire Cowper	30

"	Puerto Rican	45
"	Scottish American	30
"	Silja	29-32, 36,38
"	Speedwell	38
"	St.Elstan	43,44
"	Strathcarry	47
"	Sulla	29, 31,32,40,41,75
"	Sumba	28,30,36,38,40,73,75

Allied Escort Vessels

H.M.S. Avenger		21
"	Beagle	43
"	Bergamot	44
"	Bermuda	43

German vessels.

Made in the USA
Charleston, SC
13 June 2016